Child Abuse

THE FAMILY

CHILD ABUSE

by
Jonathan Bliss

The Rourke Corporation, Inc.

The Rourke Corporation, Inc.
P.O. Box 3328, Vero Beach, FL 3296490-8726

Bliss, Jonathan.
        Child abuse / by Jonathan Bliss.
            p.   cm — (The Family)
        Includes bibliographical references and index.
        Summary: Defines what child abuse and incest are, why it happens, and what you can do about it.
        ISBN 0-86593-081-3
        1. Incest—United States—Juvenile literature.   2. Child abuse—United States—Juvenile literature.   3. Incest—United States—Prevention—Juvenile literature.   4. Child abuse—United States—Prevention—Juvenile literature.
        [1. Child abuse.   2. Incest.]   I. Title   II. Series: Family (Vero Beach, Fla.)
        HQ72.U53B57   1990
362.7'6—dc20   90-36442
                                                                                CIP
                                                                                 AC

Series Editor: Gregory Lee
Editors: Elizabeth Sirimarco, Marguerite Aronowitz
Book design and production: The Creative Spark,
    Capistrano Beach, CA
Cover illustration: Rob Court

Child Abuse

Contents

I. I Don't Wanna Talk About It

Cindy

The other kids in Cindy's class talk about sex a lot and think about it constantly. All the time it's as if sex were something cool and forbidden, like buying a new dress on your mother's credit card without her knowing. The boys boast about a cheerleader or date they've kissed or "almost made it with." Cindy's girlfriends talk about cute boys and what it must feel like to kiss Tom Cruise. Cindy always smiles and tries to be part of the group. But sometimes when she's with her friends, she realizes she's not like them. After all, they weren't having sex with their father when they were ten years old.

Cindy's father started sneaking into her bedroom at night when she was four. First he just touched the private parts of her body. Later though, when she was ten, he started having sex with her. Usually it happened when

•
A seven-year-old girl hides in the "house" she has made. When their home life is a nightmare, children sometimes try to create one that they can control.
•

he'd been drinking, but since he drank all the time, it happened often. She cried at first and begged him not to do it. He told her to be quiet, not to tell her mother. Besides, he told her it was all her fault.

Once, she tried to tell her mother what her father was doing, but she wouldn't listen. Instead her mother just screamed at her, told her she was a liar, and ran away crying. Then her father beat her. After that, she pretended she was asleep whenever her father slipped into her bed. But that didn't stop him. Nothing did.

Cindy doesn't want to think about it now. It's embarrassing not to be like everyone else, to realize that there's something really different about you. Lately, things are beginning to go wrong. She's doing badly in school. Once she used to be a B+ student; now she's flunking English and Math cold, not paying attention in classes. She's not eating and what she does eat she throws up. There are circles under her eyes and her arms look like twigs. At the strangest times she starts to cry about nothing, and she gets angry at the smallest things.

Most of her friends avoid her since she's started acting so weird, especially when boys are around. She uses bad language and loses her temper. For quite a while now, she's thought about running away, or maybe doing something a little more permanent.

Scott

Scott can't remember the last time there weren't bruises some place on his body. Most of the time, he's covered with them. In the locker room, kids used to ask him where the bruises came from, and he always told them from football or basketball or falling down the stairs. It wouldn't be cool to tell them his father did it.

It usually starts with his father screaming at his mother and goes on from there.
Scott's mother used to try to stop it, but by
now she's too beaten up herself to stop
him. She cringes and whimpers whenever
his father starts yelling. Scott tries to stop
his father from hurting his mother and his
younger brothers, but his old man is strong
and gets wild when he's angry. It would
take a crowbar to stop him once he starts
screaming. The only thing anyone can do is
run the other way or get down and cover
up. Scott doesn't want to talk about any of
this. He used to think every father acted
like his old man, but now he knows better.
When Scott acts like his father at school,
beating up the smaller kids, they call him a
bully and a coward and send him to the
principal's office.

A few times the principal brought in a
social worker to ask him some questions.
But Scott always says the same thing: "It's
nothing. I don't wanna talk about it." It's
nobody's business but his own, just like his
mother told him. It's embarrassing. And he
doesn't want to be the one who breaks up
the family. Besides, his father has threatened to kill him if he ever tells the police.

Child Abuse And Incest

Child abuse and incest. Chances are
you're reading this book because you're curious
about the words "child abuse" and "incest," or
you think someone you know has this problem.
Perhaps you yourself are a victim and want to
know more about it. Whichever it is, you have a
right to know what kind of behavior is considered to be wrong. Don't let anyone tell you dif-
ferently. And don't listen to people who tell you
that this is a dangerous, sinful, or forbidden

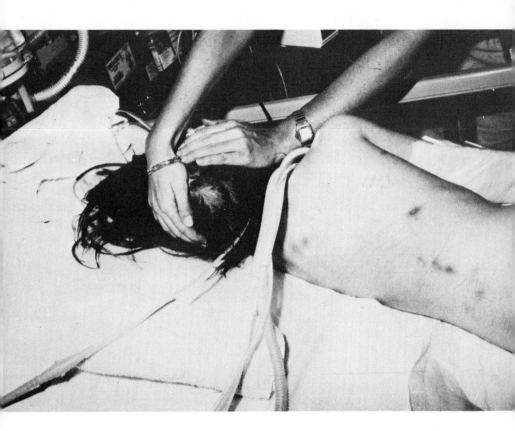

A police photograph of six-year-old Lisa Steinberg, a New York girl who lapsed into a coma and died after a severe beating by her guardian. The Steinberg murder case drew nation-wide attention to the horrors of child abuse.

subject. It isn't. Child abuse and incest are *very* common problems today. Not that you could tell Cindy or Scott that. They think they have some rare, incurable disease, like leprosy. In fact, that's only half the problem. They're also filled with shame, anger, and confusion. They think the problem is their fault. They're afraid if they tell someone about it, that person will think they're different or weird. They're also afraid that if their parents found out they told, they would get angry and punish them. And there's always the chance their family would be destroyed.

Most victims of abuse or incest think they're totally alone, and that nobody understands their problem. They think they should keep their mouths shut about what's happening to them.

They're wrong. They should know that millions of people in the United States have been victims of incest and child abuse. Many are hiding the same secrets, hating themselves the same way, feeling guilty about the same things, and carrying around memories no one should have to bear.

This book will tell you what abuse and incest are, why it happens, and—most important—what you can do about it. Some of it is pretty hard to read, but you'll get through it. You can handle the truth.

II. What Are Child Abuse And Incest?

When parents make their child "clean the plate," it does not necessarily mean that they are guilty of child abuse.

Being young isn't easy. Everywhere you look there are rules: how to dress, how to act, what to learn, who to play with, what time to be home for dinner—and exceptions to the rules. Just when you think you've learned all the rules, someone tries to change them.

Even your parents and their friends can act this way. When people keep changing the rules on you, it's called *inconsistent behavior*. For example, inconsistent is when a father congratulates his son for getting an A in math, then makes fun of him for

·15·

being a nerd. Or a mother who hugs you one moment, then smacks you across the face the next. When people can't seem to make up their minds how to act toward you, you don't know how you should act toward them. Sometimes this inconsistency is part of life, but sometimes it's part of abuse. Someone might tell you that they like you or love you, then do things to you that no one would ever do if they really liked you or loved you.

Ideally, parents are supposed to protect their children and help teach them about the world so they can grow up to become good, kind people who will raise good, kind kids. The problem is, many people can't seem to get it right. They get angry. They get drunk. They lose control. They get crazy. They do terrible things. Sometimes they beat or molest their kids, or even other people's kids, often because they were beaten or molested when they were children. Adults sometimes do things to children they would never be able to do to other adults.

Maybe you're still unsure what abuse really is. Let's look at some examples, like spanking, for instance. Is spanking abuse? It can be, when it goes

So What Exactly Is *Child Abuse*?

It's often defined in the textbooks as:
Damage to a child for which there is no reasonable explanation. Child abuse includes non-accidental injury, neglect, sexual molestation, and emotional abuse.
What do these big words mean?
• **Non-accidental injury** means when someone hurts you on purpose. If a parent or stranger beats you again and again, that's non-accidental.
• **Neglect** means when the person responsible for protecting you refuses to feed you, clothe you, send you to school, or protect you. Sometimes parents lock children in a room and don't feed them or let them go to the bathroom for days. That is child neglect.
• **Sexual molestation** means when a parent or stranger touches the private parts of your body or has sex with you. For example, when an adult, friend, teacher, or stranger forces you to do sexual acts with them, that is sexual molestation.
• **Emotional abuse** means that someone is trying to make you feel terrible about yourself by telling you that you're no good or evil or stupid, when it isn't true.

too far. By law, only a few people, like your parents, have the right to spank you. Parents usually spank children to punish or discipline them. Parents usually set limits or laws for their children, and if the children disobey, the parents may spank them. When parents hit children for no obvious reason, or because they *feel* like hitting them, this is child abuse. More than half the parents in this country admit to spanking their children, but most will say they rarely do it.

There are other kinds of violence that aren't normal, like kicking, biting, beating, or attacking with knives or guns. What parents and other adults cannot do is force you to do things that make you feel bad about yourself, make you unhappy, or hurt you.

Is being beaten by a parent or another adult really child abuse? Most of the time, yes. No one has the right to hurt or injure you. An occasional spanking is one thing. Hitting you in the face, whipping you with a belt, or starving you is quite another. These are all physical abuse.

No one has the right to touch you in places where you don't want to be touched—*no one.* Not a stranger, not a friend, not even your parents. No one has the right to force you to have sex or do sexual things with them. That's called sexual abuse.

Is it okay for an adult to force you or coax you into having sex? No. *Never.* Sex is something very special between people. It is something you should enjoy when you reach the right age. It should be one of the most exciting and pleasant experiences in your life. But in order for both people to feel good about it, both people must say "yes" to sex in advance. If only one person wants to have sex and the other person doesn't, then sex shouldn't happen. If you don't know about sex, or if you aren't prepared for sex, then you shouldn't have it. And if anyone tries to convince you to have sex and you don't want to, *tell them you don't want to and leave.* If anyone even tries to force you to have sex, they are abusing you.

Having Sex

What does "having sex" mean? *Foreplay* and *intercourse* are two words that describe having sex.

Foreplay means serious kissing, both on the lips and on other parts of the body, including the breasts and genitals; it may also mean someone else touching and rubbing your genitals (the penis and testicles, if you're male; the vagina, if you're female).

Intercourse refers to the act of penetration (sometimes called *copulation*) by a penis, whether the person being penetrated is female or male. If the sexual contact involves a male's penis entering a female's vagina, this is called *heterosexual* intercourse. If sex occurs between two men or two women, this is *homosexual* intercourse. If the contact occurs between people in the same family—such as a father and daughter, mother and son, father and son, uncle and niece, grandfather and granddaughter, or sister and brother—this is called *incest.*

If intercourse occurs between two adults who want to have it and aren't related to each other, this is usually considered normal sexual activity, whether it be heterosexual or homosexual. The law won't object, even if some people or religions do. If one person forces another person into sex, this is considered *rape.* Rape is definitely wrong, and definitely against the law.

If either foreplay or intercourse occurs between an adult and a child, this is considered sexual abuse or *molestation.* If it takes place between a child and either one of his/her parents or brothers/sisters, this is called incest. Rape, sexual abuse, molestation, and incest are all acts which are against the law and can be punished.

For a moment, let's go beyond lawful or unlawful. The real test of whether something is right or wrong is whether an act hurts someone. This is the best way a person can tell whether things they do are basically good or bad. You've heard the phrase, "Do to others as you would have them do to you." This means that if someone wants to have sex with you, make sure you know what you're getting yourself into. Make sure that you approve of doing it, and that you won't hurt the other person by taking part.

Was this true of Cindy's father who had intercourse with her? Who was this act good for? Not the father, who was abusing his daughter. Not Cindy, who was the victim of her father's abuse. Not the mother, whose husband was abusing her daughter. No one benefitted. Under all circumstances, incest is wrong.

Or what about Scott? Scott's father beat his wife and children. Was this right? Absolutely not. Beatings hurt the victims both physically and emotionally. Every year, thousands of children, even tiny babies, *die* from beatings, usually given by their parents. Sometimes beatings and sexual abuse happen at the same time. There is nothing about either sexual abuse or physical abuse that is good or acceptable behavior, although as you'll read in the next chapter, it is a very common occurence.

III. The Shame
Of History

Incest has a long history. You can even read about it in the Bible. For example, Moses was born from the union of his nephew and his aunt (Num. 26:59). Abraham was married to his paternal sister (Gen. 20:12), and Jacob married two sisters (Gen. 29:21). And who else did the children of Adam and Eve have to marry but each other? At the same time, the Bible does specifically forbid incest and abuse in Leviticus, as well as other places.

Other cultures and religions also have a history of incest and abuse. Most past civilizations had to deal with incest and physical abuse. The Babylonian, Greek, Jewish, Chinese and Japanese cultures all had laws against it. You can find examples of sexual and physical abuse in the history of

A counselor answers a call on a "domestic violence" hotline. Battered women and their children can find temporary housing at shelters nationwide by calling for help. Hotlines offer free counseling and support.

different countries. In ancient Greece, the only kind of relationship thought to be truly noble and loving was that between a man and a young boy (sometimes called *pederasty*). No less a figure than the great philosopher Plato maintained that the love between two men was superior to the love between a man and woman, although what Plato called "real love" was largely spiritual and non-sexual—what we call "platonic" love today.

Children as Property

Children throughout history have also been routinely abused, even murdered, without the abusers being punished. Why is this? Because until the last 50 or 100 years, children weren't valued very highly. All the ideas people have today about how special a baby is, how important a child's upbringing is, weren't thought about back in 1266 or 1620 or 1745. In poor families, a child was just another hand to help in the fields, cook the food, or help protect the family property. They were more like commodities, like a cow or an acre of land. In rich families, children were used to make good marriages for the benefit of the family name. A parent often couldn't afford to invest much time or love in children because so many of them died young. There were few cures for disease, and life was hard.

There was also no such thing as a "childhood" as we know it today. Children were considered to be young adults until they reached the age of ten or eleven, and then they were considered adults. If you look at old paintings, you'll see that most children were dressed just like adults. Even child princes and princesses were expected to act like adults. If they didn't, they were sometimes beaten "for their own good." In fact, parents often believed their children were being brought up "properly" when they were punished frequently.

A good example of this was King Louis XIV of France, one of the great kings of Europe in the 17th century. When he was growing up, his father, King Louis XIII, encouraged his son's teacher to beat him regularly "for his own good."

History tells us that violence was common, almost normal. Public executions and torture were not only approved by the general public, but served as entertainment. For instance, thousands of Romans used to fill the Colosseum to see men kill each other in gladiator contests, or to see wild animals tear Christians apart. In 16th-century Spain, large crowds gathered to cheer as non-Christians were burned alive at the stake. In England before 1800, a crowd could always be found at the spectacle of a criminal being beaten, hanged, or tortured to death. Even today, people still seem to find violence entertaining. We pay boxers millions of dollars to beat each other up, and many are avid watchers of violent sports like football and hockey. Our fascination with horror and "slasher" movies and the violence we can watch on television are simply new ways of experiencing violence in our "civilized" society.

Sex and Psychiatry

As for sexual abuse in history, there aren't any reliable statistics, although we know that until recently women and children had few laws to protect them. Even as late as the early 1900s Sigmund Freud—the father of psychiatry—didn't believe his female patients who told him they had been molested by their fathers. Freud thought these women were either lying or imagining things. His explanation, called the *Electra Complex*, was that all women secretly wished to have sex with their fathers, and that some even *imagined* that they had. Of course, said Freud, such a thing couldn't really be happening. What father would have sex

with his daughter, or mother have sex with her son? It was unthinkable! No one in nice, civilized Vienna, Austria (where Freud lived) would think of doing something so awful! Most doctors at that time agreed. How could something that everyone believed was wrong really be happening?

Polynesia, among other places, used to have "sexual initiation rites" for their young people. Two hundred years ago, for example, the natives of Tahiti initiated a girl into adulthood by having another member of the tribe have sex with her. Even today, there is a tribe in Borneo that doesn't allow boys to become men until they have had sex with an older male member of the tribe. In India, girls 13 years old or younger are married to much older men, and are expected to have sex with them as soon as they are physically capable. But Borneo, Tahiti, Polynesia and India are not like America, right? Think again. You don't have to look any further than American history for cultures that approved of sex between adults and children. For instance, the Oneida group was a religious society in the Middle West in the late 1800s that insisted, as one of their laws, that each girl or boy member be introduced to sex by an older member of the opposite sex. But most people in society paid little attention to these "exceptions." Since sexual abuse and incest were forbidden, they didn't officially exist.

It wasn't until the 1960s and 1970s that some people began thinking the experts had been wrong about the occurrence of incest. Using surveys and interviews, a new class of professionals called *sociologists* started putting together some alarming statistics. It soon became obvious that abuse and incest were more than just minor problems. Abuse was going on everywhere, in every country, every state, every city, and at every level of society.

IV. The Numbers And The Problem

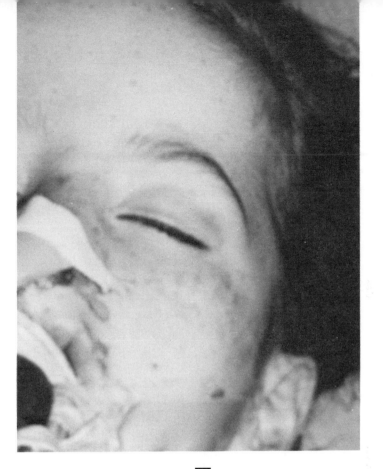

Jessica

When Jessica was ten, her father died. Her mother worked at a dry cleaners to earn a living, but between her two brothers, Jessica, and her mother, there was never enough food in the house. About a year after her father died, Jessica's mother remarried. From the beginning, her new stepfather acted strangely toward Jessica—kind of seductive. He was always nice and sweet when her mother was in the house, but when she left to go to work, the stepfather started coming on to her.

He would make Jessica sit with him at the kitchen table and listen to him complain about how hard it was to find a job, and what "bastards" men were who didn't understand his

Children are often
abused by adults
because they cannot
fight back.

problems. He always ended up by asking Jessica whether any boy had ever been a "bastard" to her. When she asked him what he meant, he said, "you know, touching you in places you don't want to be touched." Even then, Jessica guessed what he was getting at. When he started showing her what he meant, she became afraid.

Slowly, his demonstrations of what boys shouldn't do to her became more detailed. He started fondling her, asking her if it felt good. She felt guilty because it did feel good, sort of. She also felt scared, because she didn't want him to do it, and yet she didn't know how make him stop. When he warned her not to tell her mother, Jessica was sure what he was doing was bad. One day, her mother had to leave to go stay with her sick sister. Jessica pleaded with her not to go, knowing what would happen, but her mother told her she was being silly.

That night, her stepfather came to her room and had sex with her for the first time. It hurt a lot and Jessica was terrified. Each night after that, her stepfather had intercourse with her. Even after her mother returned, he continued to have sex with her whenever he could. At last Jessica couldn't stand it any longer and told her mother, but her mother didn't believe her. She called Jessica "a liar." What was Jessica trying to do, her mother yelled, break up the family? Then her mother told her stepfather. When he heard what she'd said, he became very angry and threatened to kill her if she ever told anyone else. Scared, ashamed, and lonely, she decided to run away. In her mind, there was no other choice.

Statistics On Sexual Abuse

One out of every *three* girls is sexually abused before she reaches age 18. One out of every *eleven* boys is sexually abused. At least half

of these attacks occur within the family. Physical abuse, like beatings, are just as common: one of every ten children will be beaten badly enough during the course of his or her first 16 years to require medical help.

This means that the chances of a girl being sexually or physically abused *by a member of her own family* are greater than her chances of going to college. Some experts think more than half of all girls over the age of eight will have some kind of sexual contact with an adult *before* they reach puberty.

If you are a boy, you're more likely to be

Children who are victims of incest may not show any outward signs of a problem. The scars are on the inside.

physically or sexually abused as a child than you are to play a varsity sport in high school. As many as 25 percent of all reported childhood sexual molestations involve boys.

It is estimated that as many as 250,000 children in the United States are sexually molested in their homes every year. Seventy-five percent of these incidents take place between fathers and daughters. Look at these statistics. They should tell you something about the size of the abuse problem. Physical and sexual abuse are *very* common.

Researchers who study the abuse problem have recently provided data about a frightening new aspect of the abuse problem: satanic and ritualistic abuse. There are groups in this country—some experts believe *many* groups—that practice sexual or physical abuse. Some call themselves religious organizations; others are secret cults that worship the devil. What many of these groups have in common is the abuse of children, either as a means of teaching child obedience to the group, or as a way of initiation.

A Disturbing Trend

Doctors and social workers are beginning to see more and more children who have been victims of these disturbed people. Some of the victims have parents who are members of cults and have willingly given their children to be abused. Other victims have been kidnapped and used as part of secret rituals that include sacrifices. Some of these victims are made to witness acts of violence, like the killing of an animal, and then forced to commit the same act of violence. Other victims are punished for any deviation from the group's rules. Still others are forced to participate in sexual activities with adults or other children.

While this may all sound like something out of a Steven King novel, there are in fact many groups in the United States today that routinely abuse children in the name of God or Satan or some other deity. There are even some organizations that openly support the use of children for sexual activities. One of these organizations claims to have as many as 3,000 members!

Don't think these kinds of things only happen to poor or disadvantaged people. It's not true. Sexual abuse can happen in any house, any neighborhood. The abuser can be rich or poor, any color, and belong to any religion. Sexual abusers can be friends, parents, teachers, lawyers, professional athletes, politicians, or even doctors. The problem is found in every social class.

Look at your own school, for example, at your friends and classmates. This may sound shocking, but as many as half of all the kids in your school may have had some experience with abuse, either because they know someone who has been abused, or because they have been abused themselves in some way. Impossible? Wouldn't you be able to recognize your abused classmates? Not necessarily. Often they don't look or act any different from anyone else. They're just like you. They act the same, dress the same, even talk the same. They're what you'd call "normal." But they're also abused.

Many are probably like Jessica. They believe that there is no one to talk to, that no one will listen or understand them, and that it's not cool to be different. So they hide the truth. You wouldn't be able to spot Jessica either. She acts like every other kid in school. In fact, she's probably just like *many* other kids in school who have been abused.

V. It Doesn't Bother Me

T ony

While other 11-year-old boys think about buying a better skateboard or going to rock concerts with the guys, Tony has different concerns. He's become a real pain to be around. Classmates accuse him of being paranoid. His teachers complain that he doesn't concentrate anymore in class, and that his grades have gone from Bs down to Ds and Fs.

He's afraid to be alone, and frightened to walk down his tree-lined street, especially at night. He worries that the same two adults who sexually molested him before will come back and hurt him again.

Even his parents are getting alarmed. It's not just that he bullies his sister. The other day

Sexual abuse can lead a child to withdraw from the everyday world.

·33·

he backed her into the bathroom and started "touching" her in places he shouldn't. His teachers reported that Tony was "acting inappropriately in class." But when Tony's parents asked him what was wrong, he stormed out of the room, and didn't talk to them for a week.

To himself, Tony can pretend that the incident didn't happen, that the two strangers who violated him that night haven't affected his life, and that if he keeps quiet the whole thing will go away. But his friends, family, and teachers know something is bothering him.

Trying To Forget

Like Tony, we often want to forget painful subjects. It's a natural way of dealing with problems too big or too tough to handle at the moment. We pigeon-hole problems and hope they'll "get lost in the paperwork." If that were true, psychologists and psychiatrists would be out of their jobs. People could just walk away from a problem and that would be that.

Unfortunately, we remember very well. We remember little things like the names of our favorite sports heroes, the name of a favorite stuffed doll, or the telephone numbers of our best friends. If we remember the small stuff so well, just imagine how hard it is to forget the big stuff. Have you ever been in a car accident, or hurt yourself? If you weren't knocked silly or didn't black out, you probably remember every detail of the event years later.

Often the only remedy for an awful experience is talking about it. Sadly, that's the last thing most victims, especially young people, want to do.

Most victims of abuse, as many as 95 percent, keep quiet. After all, who can they tell? They've learned not to trust the adults, since adults mostly are the abusers. More than that, though, they don't want to tell anyone because they're convinced that what's happened to them is shameful or sinful.

It's a fact that most children who become victims of sexual or physical abuse feel a lot of guilt about what happened to them. In some way they feel it was their *own* fault, a streak of "badness" that caused the incident (or incidents) to happen in the first place.

This is particularly true if the abuse takes place at home, where the victim is likely to believe that it was something wrong with him or her that made their parent do what they did. Why do kids believe it was their fault? Often it is because the abuse was done in secrecy, like a father sneaking into his daughter's room and telling her not to tell anyone about it, or a mother beating her son and accusing him of having asked for it.

Victimizers are often very good at making their victims feel guilty. A molester or attacker frequently accuses the person they've just molested or beaten of "making them do it." A child is made to feel that it is something in them that has caused this thing to happen.

Misplaced Love

Since a child often knows or is related to the person who has hurt them, they keep quiet because they fear losing that person's friendship or love. This is particularly true of fathers and mothers who abuse their children. Abuse can continue for years in such circumstances because the victims believe they must protect the family from shame of discovery. More often than not, they discover shame in the same way they discovered abuse—they are introduced to it by their abuser.

This brings up an interesting question. Why do victims believe anything the victimizer says? The answer is simple. Many cases of sexual and physical abuse are committed against children between the ages of three and eight—too young to know better and too small to fight back. They believe what the person is telling them simply because that person is older than they are. Most children can't fight back, or even talk back, without risking more harm.

In junior or senior high school, victims may continue to keep quiet out of habit. They realize that what has been done or is being done to them is wrong or makes them feel bad, but they think there is no escape. Perhaps they think most children live in the same kind of situation as they do.

Just because a person knows that he or she was abused, doesn't mean they act or feel different than you or me, right? Sometimes. But a sad thing about violence is that it has a way of hurting and haunting people, even long after it's over. It changes people, the way they think, feel and live. For example:

• Of the thousands of children who run away every year, most have been abused in some way by a family member or a relative.

• A survey of San Quentin Federal Prison inmates found that every inmate had been abused as a child.

• An estimated 75 percent of all teenagers involved in prostitution—both female and male—were victims of prior sexual abuse: rape, incest, and/or molestation.

• Over 50 percent of teenage sex offenders were sexually or physically abused as children. That means one out of every two people who go on to hurt other children were abused by someone else.

• Of all the sexual assaults that occur every year, more than half of the attackers were relatives or members of the victim's immediate family.

• A large proportion of mentally ill people were sexually or physically abused as children.

In spite of these statistics it is believed that only six percent (or one in 17) of molestation or abuse cases are ever reported to the police or other authorities. Despite the pain and humiliation they suffer, victims rarely report what has happened to them. They try to hide from their memories, deny that anything happened, and won't talk about it with anyone. They hope that nobody will notice, that they can just blend in with the other kids.

But things happen inside an abused child's mind. Things not easy to see unless someone is paying close attention. Behavior and personality can change. Here are a few examples.

• Inappropriate dress: wears long sleeves or high necklines regardless of the weather. Refuses to undress for gym class.

• School attendance: late for school, or arrives at school early and stays late. Often tired and may fall asleep in class.

• Physical contact: is hungry for affection but is unable to use acceptable ways of getting it. Often apprehensive and fearful of affection or physical contact, especially with an adult.

• Extreme behavior: often cries or seldom cries. Very fearful or fearless of adult authority; extremely aggressive and destructive, or unusually passive and withdrawn. Some may act like "parents" to their parents, catering to their needs or those of other adults.

• Sudden changes in conduct: bed and pants wetting, thumb-sucking, troublemaker or totally passive.

• Appearance: dirty, hair lice, skin sores; often hungry and may hide food, or takes food or lunch money from other kids. Shows signs of being underfed, like paleness, loss of weight, no energy, little or no strength or endurance. Shows obvious need for dental care or eyeglasses. May also have bruises in various stages of healing; frequent burns, welts, or broken bones from unusual "accidents"; limping or obviously painful movements that have no apparent cause.

• Learning disabilities: trouble learning or concentrating in class when intelligence tests indicate no inability to learn.

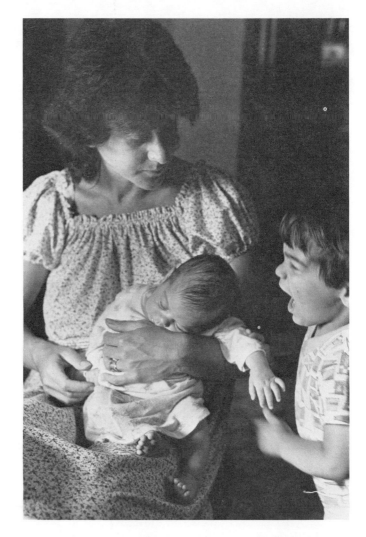

Sometimes the pressure of raising a family becomes so stressful that adults take it out on the children.

Sometimes there are even bigger changes. Memories of what has happened can be so painful that abuse victims try almost anything to blot them out. Some victims go so far as to create other personalities to help keep the bad memories locked away. Their personality literally breaks apart, leaving them with many smaller personalities to handle the difficult memories. This is called *multiple personality syndrome* (MPS), and doctors are finding that many people suffer from this disorder.

MPS can cause people to get terrible headaches, hear voices, overeat or starve themselves, lose track of time, and go into trances. Some people have the disorder so badly they can be dozens of different people housed in a single body! Imagine a person who rapidly becomes a dancer, a Russian-speaking mystic, a high-powered business-woman, a prostitute and a three-year-old child, all in the space of an hour. That's called a multiple personality. While it sounds fascinating, most of these people don't know what's happening to them, are very depressed and unhappy, and often try to commit suicide. Psychiatrists have learned that many of these MPS cases were victims of severe child abuse when they were young.

People, particularly children, can adjust to almost any environment. That's one of the remark-able things about being a human being. All people learn to live as best they can, given the situation. Children are particularly good at adapting to diffi-cult circumstances. Just think how quickly children learn a language when they are young. They learn the rules of their society just as quickly —no matter how strange those rules may be.

Children even learn to live in abusive homes, but the cost is great. Imagine that you are put in an abusive home. You are young and can't do anything to stop what's going on. You'd adapt as well as you could. You'd keep quiet and try to work in that home. Most important, you'd try to survive. But if the situation continued or got so bad that you couldn't take it any longer, you'd be faced with the same decision that many abused children face every day: run away from home, kill yourself, or live with the problem no matter how bad it gets.

There is, of course, another way to avoid or stop the abuse. That's what we'll talk about in the next two chapters.

VI. Prevention

Silvia

If you had asked Silvia when she was 16 whether she had a good home life, she would have said yes. In fact, she would tell you she was one of the luckiest girls in the world; that she loved her father and her mother; that her brothers and sisters were just the greatest; that everything was wonderful. She did well in school and was popular with the boys, she won a scholarship to college, and graduated at the top of her class. A year later, she was promoted to a high-paying position in a large corporation. It seemed like Silvia had it all and that life would be perfect, but it didn't work out that way.

Sexual abuse of children harms them physically and emotionally.

Silvia was 25 when she first tried to commit suicide. By age 27 she'd tried three more times, had slashed herself repeatedly with knives, and had finally been committed to a psychiatric hospital for her own safety.

If you ask her what's wrong, she'll tell you it's the voices inside her head, screaming at her, telling her what a wicked, evil creature she is, and how she needs to be punished for her sins. Over the past ten years she experienced frequent blackouts, during which she became other people and lived other lives. Her psychiatrists tell her she suffers from Multiple Personality Syndrome, that her creation of all these other personalities is actually an attempt to hide some terrible childhood trauma from herself.

She just shakes her head. What trauma could be so awful that it would cause such a reaction? she asks.

But more often she has the same vivid and terrible dream—the one in which her father rapes and beats her repeatedly. Her beloved father is transformed into a raving maniac.

She wants to forget this dream as nonsense, yet there is obviously something terribly wrong here, and she is beginning to believe what the doctors say: that maybe her father wasn't the man she remembers.

This chapter is especially important for you if you have never been abused. It will tell you of ways of avoiding abuse.

When we are young we want to be friendly and please other people, particularly adults. Remember that most adults are good people and would never hurt someone on purpose. However, there are also some bad adults who pretend they are good in order to hurt others. To tell them apart, you don't have to be an expert in human behavior. You just have to follow a few simple rules and believe in your own instincts and feelings.

Trust Your Own Feelings

You know when something strange is happening. It doesn't have to be something you can explain, you just know. Like when your heart starts to pound, or you get a stomachache, or you start to tremble or sweat or have trouble breathing. These are all ways your body has of telling you something is wrong. Any of these "funny feelings" can be a clue. And if the funny feelings are caused by someone following you or asking you to do something you don't want to do, including going with them, don't do it. Trust yourself.

Protect Your Body

Think of your body as a separate country with borders all around it. From history class, you know what happens whenever one country tries to step across the border of another country. It results in war or invasion. Don't let anyone you don't trust step over *your* border. That

The Rules of Prevention.

Trust your own feelings. If someone seems dangerous to you, avoid them, especially if he or she asks to take you somewhere, keeps following you, or tries to make you do something you don't want to do.

Protect your body. No one has the right to do things with or to your body that you don't want them to do.

Fight back. If attacked, either run or fight back and always scream. Don't let people hurt you if you can help it. They don't have the right. Use any means you have to stop them. That includes biting, hitting, scratching, kicking, anything you can do to stop them.

Don't trust all adults. Just because someone is bigger and older than you doesn't mean they have your best interest at heart. You have the right to question adults and say "no" to adult demands and requests.

Ask for help. If someone is trying to hurt you, or has hurt you already, get help. Most adults will want to help you.

means kissing, touching, hugging, or patting. There are lots of times when people do this as a sign of friendship or affection. That's okay as long as you *want* them to do it. But no one has the right to cross over your borderline, even in friendship, unless you want them to. Ask them not to. If they don't, fight back.

Fight Back

If you're attacked or chased, you have the right to protect yourself. It doesn't matter whether the person attacking you is a friend, teacher, parent or stranger, you have the right to run away or fight back. Of course, the smart thing to do is run, as fast as you can. Remember, you can outrun or outlast a lot of adults who are trying to chase you because you are younger and faster. Running away is always the best way of avoiding an attack.

Sometimes you can't run, especially if the attacker has already caught you. So fight. Don't try to fight fair. Fight as dirty as you can. Bite and gouge and kick and scratch and hit. Go for the attacker's weak spots: the groin (genitals), nose and eyes. Stomp on their toes. More and more young people are taking classes in self-protection. If you are interested in taking a course like this, ask your teacher or parent. Many schools now offer free classes in fighting back.

And most important, *scream.* No attacker likes to draw attention to what they are doing. They get scared when they think other people might notice what they're doing. And it doesn't matter whether they order you to stop or threaten to hurt you if you don't. The best thing in the world you can do is yell. That goes for boys as well as girls. It isn't being a wimp to protect yourself by screaming.

Just because a person is bigger or older than you doesn't mean they should tell you what to do. Of course your parents have the right to tell you things like when to be home at night, when to do your homework, when to do chores, or when to turn off the TV. These things are "house rules," even if you don't agree with them at the moment. But when an adult asks you to do something that feels bad, say "no," no matter who it is. You have the right to say "no" to any unwanted touch or display of affection. You also have the right to question an adult, especially a stranger, if he or she wants to hug or kiss or touch you. You don't have to be insulting, just direct.

Ask For Help

If you are attacked or hurt, ask for help. Most people will want to help a young person. Most people in our society really dislike people who take advantage of young people, and will help if you ask them.

What should you do if an attack has already taken place or if the abuse is still continuing? We will deal with that in the next chapter.

VII. Doing Something About It

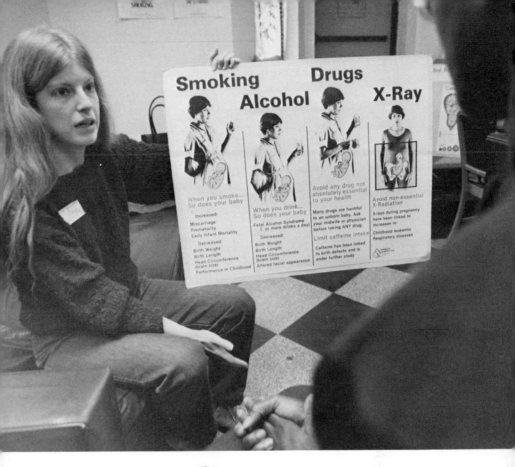

Charles

Ever since Charles can remember, his father has been drunk every Friday and Saturday night and beaten everyone in the house. Sometimes he also got drunk on Monday, Tuesday, Wednesday and Thursday nights too. Because Charles was the oldest child, he came in for the most abuse. His father's favorite trick was to take a belt with steel studs in it and whip Charles across the back. After years of this, Charles' back was a solid mass of scars.

A number of times he begged his mother to leave his father, but she always refused because she was afraid her husband might try to kill her if she tried to leave. She was also

•

Some mothers have been accused in the courts of abusing their babies even before they are born. Proper counseling to help expectant mothers during pregnancy can get their children off to the right start.

•

•47•

frightened about money. How would she make ends meet without her husband's income?

Withdrawn and shy, Charles only became more shy and distant as he became a teenager. Though he was a good student, he had trouble relating to his classmates and had no girl-friends. He stayed away from home as much as possible and only went back to change his clothes and check up on his mom and brother.

One night he made the mistake of coming home too early. His father was still there, drunk. He'd already beaten Charles' mother unconscious and was just starting on Charles' younger brother when Charles came into the room. His father turned to charge at him, his eyes wild. Something snapped inside Charles. In a rage, he picked up a kitchen knife and stabbed his father twenty times in the chest. The next thing Charles knew, his father was dead and the police were there.

Six months later, Charles was found inno-cent of murdering his father. The jury ruled it "justifiable homicide." Now he has the difficult task of putting his life back together after so many years of violence.

Sometimes, nothing you can do will stop the abuser. Maybe you don't have time to run away. Maybe you are too small or too young to know what to do. Maybe it's a parent or brother or relative who is hurting you. Once abuse has start-ed, you need to know how to stop it or do some-thing to help you deal with it. But there are other ways to stop an abuser besides the drastic way Charles did it.

An abuse problem is not going to go away by itself. Without help, neither the abuser nor the situation causing the abuse are going to change. Even after the abuse is over, you still have to live with memories of the abuse, and this usually requires some kind of professional help.

There are many abused young people who think they can make things all right by keeping quiet. But if statistics say anything, they say that the victim will suffer in the end. The only person who is helped by having the victim stay quiet is the abuser. He or she is counting on the fact that the victim will be too scared or too ashamed to tell anyone what's happened.

Talk To Your Parents

If you have been abused, you should seek help. You must tell someone about the problem before they can help you. You have to tell them why you need help so they can do something to protect you. You have to tell someone, the question is, *who?*

Sometimes the answer is easy. If you're abused by someone *outside* your family, then you tell someone *inside* your family. Mom or Dad should be your first choice. Parents may be shocked to hear what you tell them, but they'll probably listen to you. Don't be afraid to tell your parents if the person who hurt you is a relative or friend of the family. Since your protection and comfort is their responsibility, a parent is the best person to ask for help.

Things get harder if the abuse is committed by someone from your immediate family. Now you have to decide who you can trust.

Don't try to accuse the abuser. They are much too disturbed, addicted, or indifferent to know what harm they're doing. Other times, they know what they're doing, but they like it too much to stop. It would be easy if you could just tell them to stop and that would solve the problem. But problems like drinking or drugs are vicious habits, and they take a long time to cure.

However, you may be able to tell your *other* parent. Sometimes this works. They may be strong and tough enough to handle the truth. If they believe what you are saying is true, they might do something about stopping it. But sometimes they are part of the problem. Many wives of abusive husbands, for example, are too frightened to admit that anything is going on. They are often women who come from a background of abuse themselves. They don't feel capable of stopping the abuse of their children. They may be too frightened, too dependent, or too used to being hurt themselves to help somebody else. While one usually thinks of a mother as someone who protects her children from harm, a surprising number of mothers in abusive households deny that anyone is being harmed. It's difficult to admit that something bad is happening in their own family. Many children tell of mothers who, when told of the abuse, accuse the victim of lying or beg the abused child not to tell anyone because it would "hurt the family" or make the father angry. So if your mother or father doesn't want to help you, find someone else.

Talk To Another Family Member

Sometimes another member of the family can help, like an older brother, a grandparent, or an aunt or uncle. But be careful here, especially if the relative is related to the abuser. Remember that a large percentage of abusive parents were raised in abusive households, and it is possible that another family member might be more interested in keeping the abuse quiet than protecting the victim. But if you feel you can trust another member of the family or a relative, mention the problem to them and see what they do.

Your best bet, however, is to tell someone outside the house, like a teacher or policeman.

Talk To Someone At School

Teachers are educated to the symptoms and

signs of abuse, and they know how serious and widespread the problem is. They won't send you to the principal or call your parents. Instead, they will try to get you in touch with people who can help you. And they *will* listen.

Other people you can talk to are the school nurse, school social worker, or student counselor. Most schools today have a school nurse who visits several times a week. They can be very helpful since they are trained to deal with abuse victims.

Talk To The Police

The police can also help. They aren't all guns and badges. Sometimes the most understanding person of all can be a policeman or policewoman. Special detectives are assigned to handling abuse cases. They have been trained to be quiet about the whole thing and get you to people who can help you the most. Either talk to the police who patrol your neighborhood, or look in the telephone directory under "Police" and ask for a detective from the "child abuse" or "human services" division.

Use Your Phone Book.

You can look in the Yellow Pages of your phone book for names and telephone numbers of many organizations and people who help abused or battered children. Look first under these listings:

Child Abuse and Neglect
Clinics
Human Services Organizations
Crisis Intervention Service
Social Service Organizations.

You should be able to find the names of many organizations under these listings that can help you.

Other Places To Get Help

If you still need someone who specializes in abuse, at the back of this book is a list of organizations that are expert in treating abuse victims. All of them have people who are helpful and caring.

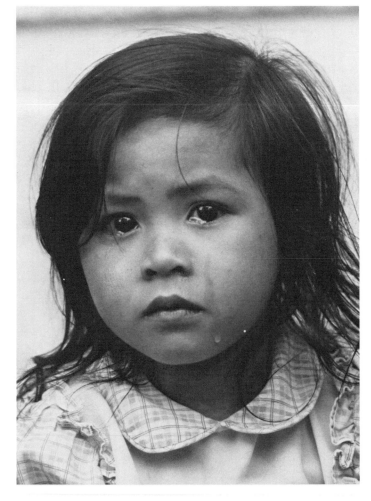

They won't embarrass you or stir up a lot of trouble. All of these organizations are free. Some may not have an office in your area, but others have offices all over the country where you can call. Some even have "800" numbers which are free (and don't show up on telephone bills). There is at least one of these organizations you can reach from wherever you are.

In addition, almost every county and city in the country has people assigned to handling the problem of child abuse. They can often direct you to the best local resource. Look in the white pages of your telephone book, just before the "A" listings, where all the government pages are. First, look under "Child Protective Services." Then look under "Health and Human Services," "Human Services," or "Health Care." Under one of these titles you should find a department for "Child Health." Also look under "Family Support." (When trying to get help from a government agency, it sometimes takes a while to find the right person to talk to. Don't give up. Any government operator should be able to refer you to the department that handles child abuse.)

If you need more resources, look in the white pages under "Rape Crisis Centers" or "Crisis Intervention Services." These groups handle all sorts of problems, from rape and incest to battered children and adults. Once again, almost every part of the United States has such a center or service.

Most of all, don't be afraid or embarrassed to call. Many people call everyday. Nobody needs to know that you made the call. The most important thing is to first tell someone what has happened to you, and then work with those who can help you to start feeling good about yourself.

VIII. Abuse And
The Law

Nancy

It took Nancy almost 25 years to tell any-one that she had been sexually and physically abused by her stepfather. It happened between the ages of six and 12, but even at 32 she still bore the emotional scars of her experience.

The people she told were her mother and stepfather. In a 17-page letter, she exposed her stepfather's history of abuse. It shocked Nancy's mother so much that she filed for divorce. Eventually, both Nancy and her sister testified in court about being abused by their stepfather. He tried to deny everything, but his nervousness made it clear to everyone in the courtroom that he was lying. The judge sen-tenced him to three years in jail.

•

The McMartin Preschool molestation case was the longest criminal trial in U.S. history. Raymond Buckey, right, was acquitted of 52 counts, but was re-tried on several other counts in 1990.

•

Sometimes you have to deal with the law. Many cases of abuse can be handled quietly, but if the abuser continues to hurt people, the law must step in. Don't be afraid of the law. It is there to help and protect you and all victims.

Only five years ago, the law and lawyers didn't know the best way to treat abuse victims. A lot of time was taken up with courtroom appearances, and questioning could be very embarrassing. But like so much else connected with this problem, things have changed.

Now there are special legal programs for abuse victims. In witness and child advocacy programs around the country, abused children are interviewed in a calm setting by trained social workers and psychologists. Their testimony is taken, and they are helped by the legal system. Working through these programs, a child may never have to go to court at all (or they may testify on videotape). If a victim must go to court, he or she is assured that it won't happen more than once or twice. The victim is protected by the program from the kind of questioning that used to make things so difficult for the victim.

Sometimes the victim must be examined by a doctor. It is the doctor's job to check the victim for signs of abuse. This is just like going to any family doctor or clinic.

If the abuser is a parent of the victim and the victim feels the only way to get away from the abuse is to get away from the abuser, the law can help by placing the victim in another home or finding a "halfway house" where the victim can stay until things get better at home. The victim may still choose to live with his or her parents if the abusing parent agrees to stop the abuse and seek help for the problem. If the problem doesn't stop, other steps have to be taken.

Keep in mind that the goal of the law is to keep the abuser from abusing. That doesn't always mean putting the abuser in prison. Most of the time it means putting them into special help programs that try to keep them from doing it again. Victims who are afraid that they will be sending someone like a father or an uncle to jail should know that imprisonment usually doesn't happen unless the abuse has been very bad. But there have been cases where the abuser did go to prison. For example, anyone who has raped or beaten or molested a lot of children over a long period of time usually goes to jail. Whether they stay there long enough is another issue.

In the Courts

You may have heard about the famous child abuse case in the 1980s called the McMartin molestation case. The McMartin family ran a preschool where children and parents said that the McMartins and other teachers abused and molested the children. The case went to trial and became the longest-running, most expensive trial in the history of the American court system. When it was over, the case had lasted six years and cost $8 million. The McMartins were found not guilty. The trial showed how expensive and time-consuming child abuse cases can sometimes be.

Because of overcrowding in U.S. jails, sex offenders sometimes get out of prison before their full sentence is up. In fact, the average sex offender spends no more than a few years in jail before getting out. In California alone, there are more than 30,000 sex offenders out of jail and on parole. Most are supposed to check in with their parole officer every week, but it is hard for any system to keep track of that many people. Sometimes sex offenders commit more crimes and must be sent to jail several times before the law recognizes them as untreatable and keeps them in prison. Meanwhile, more children and adults get abused.

So why is child abuse such a big problem today? Maybe it's because child abuse has been a problem for a long time, but only now have we begun to recognize it. Add to this that there are many more people alive today who live in bigger, denser areas. When too many people live in too small an area, strange things happen—more murder, more crime, more poverty, and more child abuse.

Also, the way we live has changed. Families are less important than they used to be; parents spend less time with their children as they have to struggle harder to put food on the table. All this can lead to frustration which can lead to child abuse.

Finally, we are a more permissive society than we used to be. "Anything goes," we are often told, and many times we believe it. But while most of us understand that there are still limits as to what is acceptable behavior, many people in our society don't know, don't understand, or don't care about these limits. Some of these people have been abused themselves and believe it is okay to abuse others. Often the people they hurt are the ones they should love the most.

Hopefully it will not be long before we have longer jail sentences for child molesters, more education in schools and at home about child abuse, and more money for more social workers, psychiatrists, and other caregivers who try to prevent child abuse. Most important, we must learn to identify those people who are abusers, or potential abusers, and stop them before they hurt other people. If we can break the cycle of abuse that often passes from one generation to the next, we will be well on our way to curing the problem.

For More Information

Below are some national organizations that can give you information about abuse and where help is available.

- Adam Walsh Foundation, see local phone number
- Adolescent Hotline, (800) 231-6946
- American Association for Protecting Children, (303) 695-0811
- Child Abuse and Neglect Resource Center, see local phone number
- Child Abuse Registry, (800) 344-6000 or (800) 843-5678
- Childhelp USA, (800) 422-4453
- Child Protection Service, (800) 344-6000
- Children's Institute International, see local phone number
- National Association for the Children of Alcoholics, (714) 499-3889
- National Center for Missing & Exploited Children, (800) 843 - 5678
- National Coalition Against Domestic Violence, (202) 347-7017
- National Coalition Against Sexual Assault, (618) 398-7764
- National Committee for the Prevention of Child Abuse, (312) 663-3520
- Parents United, see local phone number

To find a place to stay away from home, look in the yellow pages under "Shelters" for a listing of shelters and halfway houses in your community.

Glossary

BATTERING. Physical assault on someone with the intention to injure or cause pain. Men who beat their wives are often called "wife-beaters" and women who are beaten in this way are called "battered wives."

CHILD ABUSE. Several kinds of harmful acts practiced by adults or other children on children, including rape, incest, molestation, and beatings.

EXPLOITATION. The act of taking advantage of someone else who cannot defend themselves because of ignorance, weakness, or physical size.

FOREPLAY. One of several acts that often precede intercourse, including kissing, hugging, and the fondling of a partner's sexual organs.

INCEST. Sex or foreplay between two members of the same family, such as between a mother and son, or father and daughter.

MOLESTATION. Any one of several acts including rape and foreplay, forced on an unwilling person.

RAPE. Forcing someone to have sex with someone else.

SEXUAL INTERCOURSE. The act of penetration, usually when a man's penis enters a woman's vagina. A variation of this, called "anal intercourse," involves the penetrating of an anus by the male penis.

STATUTORY RAPE. Sexual intercourse between two people, one of whom is under the "age of consent" (in most states, this is 16). This is a crime just like any kind of rape.

Bibliography

Caren Adams and Jennifer Fay, *No More Secrets*, Impact Books, 1981

Ellen Bass and Laura Davis, *The Courage to Heal*

A.W. Burgess, A.N. Groth, et al, *Sexual Assault of Children and Adolescents*, Lexington Books, 1978

David Finklehor & Associates, *A Sourcebook on Child Sexual Abuse*, Sage Publications, 1986

Jean Goodwin, *Sexual Abuse*

Kee MacFarlane, Jill Waterman, *Sexual Abuse of Young Children*

Florence Rush, *The Best Kept Secret: Sexual Abuse in Children*, Prentice-Hall Books, 1980

D.E.H. Russell, *The Secret Trauma: Incest in the Lives of Girls and Women*, Basic Books, 1986

Lauren Stratford, *Satan Underground*

Index

Picture Credits